Unveiled Beauty

MARITZA OLIVERAS

UNVEILED BEAUTY

Written by Maritza Oliveras

Printed in the United States of America

Table of Content

Prologue

There are many things my heart has endured. There are battles I never thought I would win. Many storms I faced that I never thought would end—until they did. In this book, I open my heart to you to walk you through all the things I had to conquer, all that I had feared and stood in the ring to fight.

Jesus made the way; therefore, there's light and hope to make it to the end and walk-in victory.

Things will get worse before they are better. Our lives may have begun inflicted by many trials and tribulations that causes deep sorrows and loses.

But…

Blessed [fortunate] are those who endure to the end. For to them there's a kingdom that awaits in Christ Jesus. Weeping may last through the night, but joy comes in the morning.

Let our hearts walk in the footprint that Jesus Christ created for us to follow to the end. His steadfast love endures forever. There's so much beauty even in the brokenness. No matter what you are going through, you are not alone. As you read each poem, you probably can relate and see your heart has spoken the same thing.

God has given each and every one of us many gifts and talents for all to utilize and share with the world. He has giving me a new beginning to a perfect end. Unveiling a beauty that comes from the freedom only Christ can give.

Life's balance is in the gifts and talents. It's a rendezvous place we can go to escape the chaos of life. It brings joy and peace into our hearts. It keeps us inspire to aspire for more. It is God's perfect gift for us to show his goodness and glory. It brings us together enjoying the fruits of the Spirit that joins us all as one beautiful body.

The enemy tries to destroy all the beauty of God's glory, but it is up to us whether we want to come above the waters as victors in Christ's story to be who we are in the image of God through the instructions our Heavenly Father has provided us.

All of us can be more than conquerors in this world. It all depends who's voice you want to hear and who's vision you prefer to focus on. It's a matter of having a vision, writing it and making it plain (Hb. 2:2).

Even when stones are thrown our way to cause stagnation or delay, or premature abortion to our goals and dreams, know that the Lord always has a better way to help us all accomplish everything. The only way to get to it, is by walking through it and laying aside all that our hearts has endured in the past and all what you think you know, in order to follow his designed plan. *"Better is the end of a thing than its beginning"* (Eccl. 7:8). The labor pains in the beginning are very painful, but at the end, joy comes.

Every experience is an opportunity to gain insight and wisdom. They become our strength to create an even better story, poetry, artwork and even a song. So, when you don't know where to go or what to do, just follow the footprint that Jesus Christ has placed in your heart. Set your heart to the things above and let that be the imprint you leave for others to follow.

"If you stop walking, there will be no footprints for others to follow."

— Maritza Oliveras

Beauty is a light in
the heart

For Eternity

~1~

Let's go to our secret place and talk.
I'm floating to heaven;
On clouds you make me walk.

The sound of your voice lights up a fire.
It's only you who gives this desire.

You said, "I love you and you are mine."
Lord, I promise to love you back for a lifetime.
I don't want time with you to waste.
Your love captivates me leaving me in a daze.

Your grace is truly enough.
Staying by my side when life gets rough.

Whenever I don't hear from you,
Scriptures and dreams aren't enough.
I miss you for as long as earth keeps us apart.
Until I am home with you,

I'll keep you close in my heart.

You have given me hope for a better tomorrow.
Each day you ease all my sorrows.
In the secret place embraced in your arms;
Feeling so secure and out of harm.

Loving each other where two agree.
Oh, how wonderful to know,

This is a forever you and I *for eternity.*

Love's Reflection

The heart never lies.
But it also sees what it wants to see.
Like a mirror reflecting every part of me.

There are many things one *cannot hide.*

I can only fool myself,
By hiding the true feelings I once felt.
There's no denying what I believe.
For the mirror never hides,

The truth of what *we prefer to see.*

Masquerading a grieving heart
From the evil war launching flaming darts.
All the wounds so deeply bleed;
Covering it all with a smile for none to see.

Looking into the mirror of my heart,

Seeing wounds not turned to scar.
Seeking for love in all the wrong places.
Filling a void with all familiar faces.

For evil has blurred the vision,
In the pains once inflicted.
In Christ my heart made a shift.

And found a *love's reflection*
More beautiful than the world could ever gift.

Crowned

Sorrows came down harder than rain.
My heart has been filled with so much pain.
I've tasted the deepest darkness.

Marking my life as if beyond repair.
Can someone deliver me from this harshness?

I have been visited by *total despair.*

Drank from the cup full of all the shed tears

And clothed this body in a gown called *fear.*

Deception spoke louder as if it were a king.

Enslaved in chains with a clipped wing.

Pain decreed to *crowned me Queen.*

It truly knows where my heart has been.

Setting my eyes upon the hill,

I cried out for the Lord to come and heal.

The light has come and made things new.

In all authority all the demons flew.

Now, the Light has crown me righteous.

With his love, nothing can divide us.

Drank from the cup full of life.

And has crowned me His Bride.

He clothed me with a better garment.

My heart is now under new management.

For Gift of Having You

When your seasons are filled with troubles,
Sadness, grief, or even doubt,
When all those things you planned on
Just aren't turning out,

Turn to Jesus in all your sorrows
He is your Rock for many tomorrows.

Look for him pass the shadow's demands
And reach out for his hand.
He will lift you up from all the burden
For he nailed all the wounds that's now hurting.

Bearing the pain of all your sorrows;
To guard you in the earthly life years.

In all things, faithful he will stay.
To guide you and help you make it through.
Giving you a new life of hope to start anew.

His suffering was a large price to pay
For gift of having you.

A Melody of Love

~9~

As he caressed my hair,
A sweet melody played in the air.

A gentle kiss placed on the forehead.
Speaking louder words that none compared.

Dancing with my Beloved all day long.
Without a doubt it is here in His arms
Where my heart knows it belongs.

His presence needs no voice.
He fills my heart with so much joy.
There's no better choice!

I've fallen so deep.
Oh, my Beloved!
How your love fills every beat
In a melody of love that flows within me.

Let this melody of love remain
Permeating within the secret walls freely.
A love piercing through all the worldly pain.

A melody of love that burns deeply
Until I'm dark skinned.

A Love That Goes On

When I'm sleeping,
When I'm awake,
When I'm weeping,
You are always there.

It doesn't matter what I go through.
It doesn't matter where I am.

You will never forsake me.
For you are my helping hand.

When I have been anxious and fearful,
When I've fallen and done wrong,
You are my heart's confidence to be peaceful.
You are the strength that keeps me strong.

In a love that goes on.

Stay with me and dine.
Break the bread to unveil my eyes.
I see in you a light that shines.
Filling my heart more than a gold refined.

In a love that goes on,

Beyond millions of sunrises
Embedded deeply within my heart.

Soul Cries

~13~

Pain spoke loudly in a secluded shout.
In darkness stranded going on for miles.
Depression has wiped away my smile,
And love came with plenty of many doubts.

Even there in my own shadow,
Truth spoke openly
All the pain I was hiding;

Like a river flowing persistently
And very intensely,
Watching myself being swept away
By the currents of my weakness
That I didn't face yesterday.

My body laid there by the river bank.
Only God I have to thank
For saving me right on time.

He has spared my life.
Alelluia!

The words my *soul cries.*

The Dagger

So many people I've met
Who came and then they left;

Prophesying a love with a *dagger* on their sleeve,

Selling themselves for silver and fame.
Placing upon me their guilt and shame.
Stuck with a pain that never leaves.

Profuse are the kisses of an enemy.

And many have *kissed me*

Like a Judas and a Joab.

Dressed as if they are Boaz.

And some coming dressed like they are Ruth.

Can I finally expose the truth?

> Their shame and guilt had me silent.
> Betrayal only left me broken and crying;
> A little more inside; a little more in time;

> From people who made me suffered *violence*.

Taking deeper steps toward the depth of shadows.

Holding up to my face the wine bottle;

Even knowing tomorrow I'll still feel the same.

Cheers to drowning all of my sorrows;

Even though they will still visit me tomorrow.

> But, for now let me not feel a thing.
> Because *the dagger* has already
> Cut me in too deep.
> Left bleeding on the ground
> Unable to swing.

Heavy Heart

Tears rapidly running down my face.
Carrying a heavy heart full of shame.

Trying to outrun my thoughts,
But ever able to win.

God knows better is the end of a thing.
But, I'm just in the beginning
Laying at the center of the ring,

Weeping loudly through the night,
Wondering if there's truly joy in the morning?

And if this battle I could ever *win.*

On my chest lays a *heavy heart.*
And every tear has wasted me away.
Would these wounds ever turn to scars?
And would love finally be here to stay?

Is this my life that was designed?
Peace and love is all my heart craves.
Can the Savior come before I resign?

Before these thoughts take me to *the grave?*

Oh Lord

You who test the minds and hearts,
Be my shield from these fiery flaming darts.

My eyes wasted away because of my grief.
I know you work all for the good.
I just have to believe.

Just say a word.

Oh Lord, please speak to me!

The enemy encamps against me fast.
Harassing and tormenting just like the last.
Oh Lord, why do you allow such thing?

Been abused since I was a kid.
Did you not see what they did?

The enemy has planted his seed.
Now the world can see his mark.
They hemorrhage and they are deep;
As if death has come to embark.

Just say a word.

Oh Lord, please speak to me!

Are you even listening?

My Greatest Treasure

Damaged,
Broken and enraged;

Stuck fighting in the ring;

Maneuvered like a puppet *in strings.*

Endured constant losses—
Homeless, abused and betrayed.

Facing endless injustices

With judgments served on a *silver tray.*

Taken for a crazy girl—
Abandon, rejected and dismissed.

To pigs I have casted my pearls,
And every snake came with their hiss.

By a King I've been established.
In His presence I am guarded—
Mind, body and soul.

His peace and His rests are my heart's pleasure.

His steadfast love is *my greatest treasure.*

Shame

A child—
Innocent and full of cheer.

Tainted one day

By hands that cursed her in *fear.*

Evil had come quite early.
Destroying her heart that once trusted.
Making life so dark and oh, so lonely;
By a man that never got busted.

Truth kept in secret for many years.
Nobody knows all the shed tears.
Locked in a room day and night.
It is dark in here— Oh, please turn on the lights!

"I love you" dressed in pretense.
By blood family who supposed to protect.
Didn't anyone know? Didn't anyone detect?
Didn't anyone have any moral sense?

Here I am living afraid and in *shame.*
Minimizing the wrong
Dismissing all my pain.

For if I keep quiet,

Perhaps nobody is to *blame.*

Shame has become a friend.
Will this shame ever come to an end?

Judgment

~25~

No one to trust, but only *God.*
Rape has become a war against the odd.
Can't even mention the name on social media.
That is really the devil's criteria.

    To hide the truth to raise an Antichrist.
    Silencing women so no one hears their cries.
    Babies and children are being sacrificed
    To worship a false god called Baal.

Everyone keeps silent afraid of retaliation.

Truth is held captive with their evil manipulation.

If only they repent and pray.

And from their wickedness turn away,

The Lord will hear and heal our land.

If only you wake up and believe.

All the darkness will finally retrieve.

Don't seek to prove God don't exist.

All because in your sin you want to persist.

Don't say you believe in God.

Yet, you haven't changed not even by a lot.

Don't get offended when you are *reproof.*

It just shows just how much you've been fooled.

God so loved the world you can't deny.

Jesus died for you and me— that is no lie.

Accept His perfect gift of grace.

Before it's too late

And *judgment* one day you face.

A Second Chance

Forced to grow up way too fast.
Living a life stuck in the past.
Going with the current flow,
Dragged into places unknown.

The enemy came with a mighty wrath.
Turning off the light that once lit my path.
Seeking for a place to rest my head.

Only finding devils wishing me *dead*.

All that my hands found to enjoy,

The foxes came to *destroy.*

Seeking ways to finally succeed.

But darkness followed and proceed.

> All things ever come without wind.
> Sinking in a hole unable to win.
> Life spinning out of control.
> Taking steps that eats your soul.

Now with sin and death I no longer dance.

Thanks to the Lord I've been given—

A second chance.

A Change of Skin

~29~

With words you talked so keen.

Ruling my mind like you're the king.

Suffered in an abusive counterfeit love.

Where has all the joy gone?

Every touch I wished to erase.

Enslaved me and trapped me in chains.

All for their stupid selfish gains.

With my heart they aimed to *play.*
With my body they had their way.
And justice never made them pay.

I want to disappear without a trace.
The truth one day everyone will face.

Right now, I am facing mine.
As the devil whispers *"Go ahead and die!"*

Haunted memories come at night.
Tormenting with such great might.

Left wanting for *a change of skin.*
Erasing the leftover marks from therein.

What's Next?

Drawing water from a dried up well.

Seeking for a thirst to *satisfy.*

Playing with the fires of hell,

Fulfilling a desire that never gratifies.

Foolishly expecting a heart to be healed.

In the shadows where secrets are hidden.

Never facing what needs to be revealed.

Always taking bites of *the fruit forbidden.*

Hearing songs pleasing to the ear;
Every melody only brought tears.
Making deals with a renegade.
Trading blessings for counterfeits made.

One life was given with a breath.
How can I manage to rip it into shreds?
Reset the clock and take baby steps.

Waiting for God to show me…

What's Next?

Save This Sheep

Four walls and a locked door.
How can I be free to be a prisoner no more?

Inflicted with guilt belonging to another;
Manipulated for truth to ever be spoken.
The shadow of fear in the eyes of my mother,

Played like a song called, *"Forever Broken."*

Tears have been my daily food.

Wasting away in my grief,

For no one ever understood.

No one ever will believe,

All that ever happened in this room.

> This is my life the devil has chosen.
> Chained to the lies that had me frozen.
> My soul cast down under a wave
> That carried me further to the grave.

My anguish, oh, my anguish!

> I writhe in pain.
> Wishing to vanish
> Before I go insane.

Darkness invites me in too deep.

So, I call out to the Lord to *save this sheep*.

A Flaming Sword

Let the cherubim stand at the door.

Place a guard with *a flaming sword.*

Just like in the garden of Eden,

Protecting a holy ground.
Come protect this heart
That is sounding a trumpet
With its cry sound.

Like *Adam and Eve,*

Dress me with your steadfast loving care.

Don't leave me here naked.

Oh, God I'm scare!

How much more? I can't take it!

I just want this pain to leave.

My heart took a turn eastward.

Seeking for what with you I already possessed.

To you at times I didn't looked toward.

This devil fooled me to *transgress.*

Taking matters in my own hand.

Losing battles that weren't mine to fight.

Is it too late to follow your will plan?

Let your Word pierce me like *a flaming sword.*

So, this wretched heart can be made right.

The Word

The Word became flesh.
Giving hope, peace and rest.
A Word piercing bones and marrow.
To give eternal life inherited in a future tomorrow.

The Word is The Way.

Healing a broken heart once betrayed.

Shattering the lies sin embarked.

Bringing light to what was dark.

The Word is The Truth.

That brings good news to the poor.

Proclaiming liberty to the captive

That leads them to Heaven's door.

The Word is The Life.

Making everything beautiful in its time.

Trials and tribulations —Oh, yes! They will come.

At the Cross Jesus said, "It is done!"

The Word is your seed.

It's living waters; Giving the life that we need.

It is a Sword against evil forces.

It is a Savior coming with an army in horses.

To put the darkness to an end for good.

A Sweet Surrender

We all fight many battles.
Holding secrets not unraveled.
A heart wounded in despair.

And many say, *"Oh, who cares?"*

Is this the world we are living
Where many souls lie dead screaming?
Many hearts have drawn cold.
Believing they are okay from the lies told.

The truth is masqueraded;
While the devil preys and betrays.
Many fighting giants of their own
Without the Savior who sits on his throne.

If they only knew, they will find *peace.*
Even when evil in the world has increased.
If only they knew, they can be set free.
Even when the furnace is turned up seven degrees.

If only they knew all this can be
Found in the humility of
A sweet surrender to the King.

Angel of Love

Walking through life,
Holding strong to forget the past.
Carrying scars and all the pain.

Only an *Angel of Love*
Can free me from the chains.
Everyone notices but never ask.
It's hard to know what lies behind the mask.

Privately tears run down my face.
Wishing things were differently,
And the pain I could erase.
Life's circumstances caused a fall.
But I made it through them all.

Trials have a funny way to unfold;
A powerful testimony to be told.
Losing always a dear friend;
Never thinking at an instant,
Their life could come to an end.

Fragile hearts holding broken pieces.
As life lays in the hand of fate.
An Angel of Love saved me
Right before it's too late.

I've been given a second chance.
Through every storm, remember to just dance.
Love harder and make things right.
Forget the past and never lose sight.
Because blessings arrive at a Heavenly time

That comes in the wings of an *Angel of Love.*

Always There!

Many are the afflictions I received.

My only hope is the promises the Lord will keep.

Keeping afloat in waters too deep.

And in His Word I surely *believe.*

He is standing there with me.

Delivering from them all!

You've always been there.

Even when my heart couldn't see it.

Through the many afflictions I've been thru,

You've always been there.

The proof is in *your glory*

From the valley you've walked me through.

You've always been there!

Always have been there!

Even when I couldn't see it.

Even if an army encamp against me,

My heart shall not fear.

Even if a war arises against me,

My heart is confident

Because you are always there!

You are *always there!*

Always there! You've always been there!

Right beside me.

Finally, I've come to see it!

Turn Things Around

If pain taught me anything,
It taught me this…

Feel the pain.

For it will build you up.

Face your fears

For they will make you strong.

Even if the process hurts,

Know that God's love has put you *first.*

Let your knees never leave the ground.

Talk to the **Heavenly Father**

It's through him your identity is found.

From the only One who is able to

Turn things around.

The One

~47~

She was a single *rose*.
Made insignificant
In the hands who had no intend of keeping her.

They were so afraid of her voice.
So, she decided to be afraid of it too.
Was this her only choice?

There's much more to her than eyes can really see.
Far more precious than rubies will ever be.

When she looked beyond the horizon,
Just beyond the shore,
She has found her freedom
With *The One* who carried her in the storm.

She finally saw what safety looks like
In the arms of *The One* in whom she believes.

In His arms she found His might
That delivered her to be *free.*

In His Hands

My heart felt the coldness of the world.
    Many voices spinning in my head with lies;
    Parading themselves and dancing in twirls.
    My heart has felt the darkness flourished spring.
    Held captive inside a wheel that forever spins.

    Seeking in the world to find a safe place.
    Only finding more pain and tears on my face.

Never went with the motions of trends.
Never wanted to be around people who only pretends.
Only seeking for a place to belong.
But only evil seems to prolong.

Loneliness and unworthiness came knocking.
Making so much noises without stopping.
And isolation made itself a comfy place
Inside all the empty rooms of my heart's space.

Hearing another knock and it was *Jesus.*
Gave me hope in a better life's season.
In His presence I found peace, joy and love.
One look into his eyes I knew I was well of.

I'm forever grateful for all he did on the Cross.
Never again needing to seek another place.

In His hands I found my home.

Deliver Me

~51~

Emotions seem to be reasonable.
But as each one rises to surface,
They are quite treasonable.

 Like a jellyfish they appear clear.
 But underneath you'll find all that adheres.
 Full of poisonous venom that only paralyzes;

Leaving you stuck in a place that *terrorizes.*

Can I have a massive shift?
Can the circumstances and emotions
Finally cease to exist?
Oh, Lord help this blind heart to see

Where love abides and the enemy flees.

Before you I cry out and kneel.

Oh, Lord send your word so I can be *healed.*

Deliver me! Oh, Lord from all this distress.
With your wind come clear all the mess.

Let my soul be brought low.

For I know it's the only way to *grow.*

Let me dance this storm in the rain.
Let me dance this battle in your reign.

A mighty one who is capable

To deliver me from them all.

About the Author

Maritza has dedicated her life to the Mission God has called her. She is helping many find their identity in Christ and walk in the wholeness of who they are. As an overcomer of mental, physical and sexual abuse, she has found purpose in helping others overcome their battles and finding freedom as she has found it in Christ.

Her poetry is a gift God has given her. Now she is able to share her gift with the world when for many years she kept it privately. Opening the doors to her heart did not come easy, but possible through the One who healed it all—Jesus Christ!